FANTASTIC BEASTS
AND WHERE TO FIND THEM

FASHION SKETCHBOOK

SCHOLASTIC INC.

ISBN 978-1-338-11681-6

10 9 8 7 6 5 4 3 2 1   16 17 18 19 20

Printed in the U.S.A.   88

First printing 2016

Book design by Erin McMahon

Illustrations by Miss Led and Lauren Mortimer

Scholastic Inc. 557 Broadway, New York, NY 10012

Scholastic UK, Coventry, Warwickshire

FANTASTIC BEASTS
AND WHERE TO FIND THEM

FASHION SKETCHBOOK

INTRODUCTION

Newt Scamander, the world's preeminent Magizoologist, strongly believes that magical creatures should be studied and protected. Newt has made this his life's mission, traveling the globe to carry out his research.

The adventure begins when Newt arrives in New York City in the winter of 1926, with nothing more in his possession than the clothes on his back and one modest leather case. But his is no ordinary case—it is also the home of a fantastic array of magical creatures.

Jacob Kowalski—who is referred to by the American wizarding community as a No-Maj because he does not have magical powers—meets Newt when they are both at a local bank. Following a misunderstanding, Jacob and Newt get into a skirmish outside the bank, and the two accidentally switch cases. Jacob gets the surprise of his life when he returns home and opens Newt's case, unwittingly unleashing many of the Magizoologist's beloved beasts.

Meanwhile, there is something dark and ferocious terrorizing New York City. It's crushing cars, blasting through walls, and shattering windows. Some No-Majs explain the unusual disturbances as strange weather, but others suspect the truth: Magic is afoot. Mary Lou Barebone, the leader of the New Salem Philanthropic Society, leads a vocal charge in alerting people about what she believes is sinister witchcraft and wizardry all around them.

As Newt searches the city for his escaped creatures, he becomes further entangled not only with Jacob, but also with two witch sisters named Tina and Queenie Goldstein, who work for the Magical Congress of the United States of America, MACUSA. Once MACUSA becomes aware of Newt's escaped creatures, they blame him for the troubles in the city.

How can Newt save himself—and his creatures—if no one will listen to the truth?

NEWT SCAMANDER

is the world's preeminent Magizoologist. He wears practical clothing because he always needs to be ready to go on an adventure to learn about and protect the magical creatures of the wizarding world.

Color and embellish Newt's outfit.

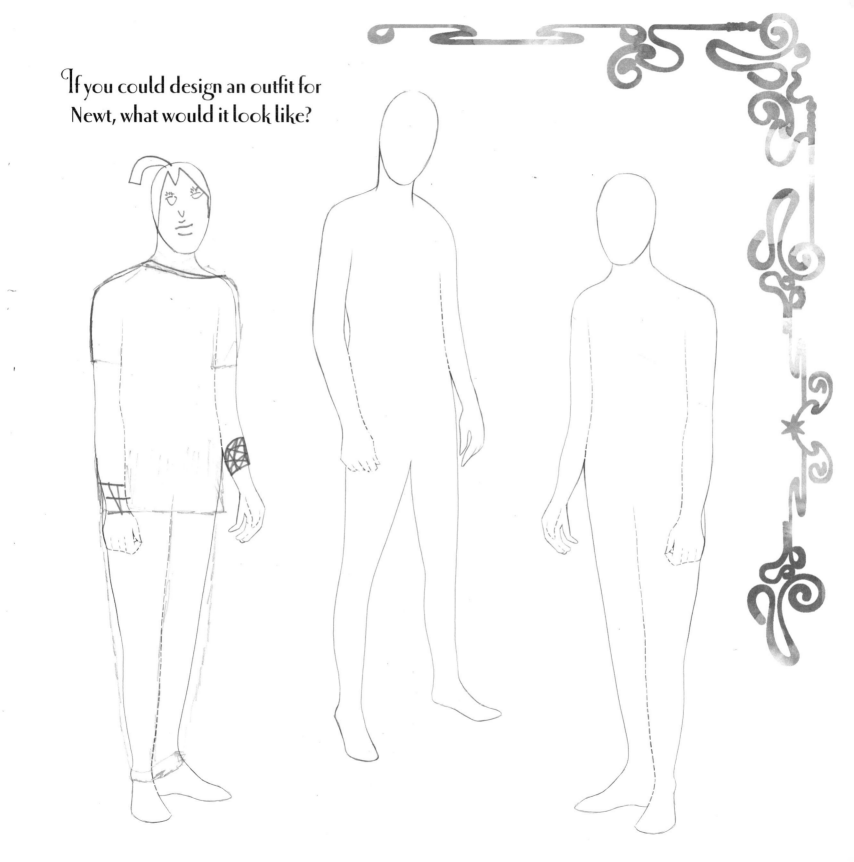

If you could design an outfit for Newt, what would it look like?

TINA GOLDSTEIN

works for the Magical Congress of the United States of America, known as MACUSA. She dresses in simple and comfortable clothing that makes it easy for her to blend into crowds of No-Majs and conduct investigations.

Color and embellish Tina's outfit.

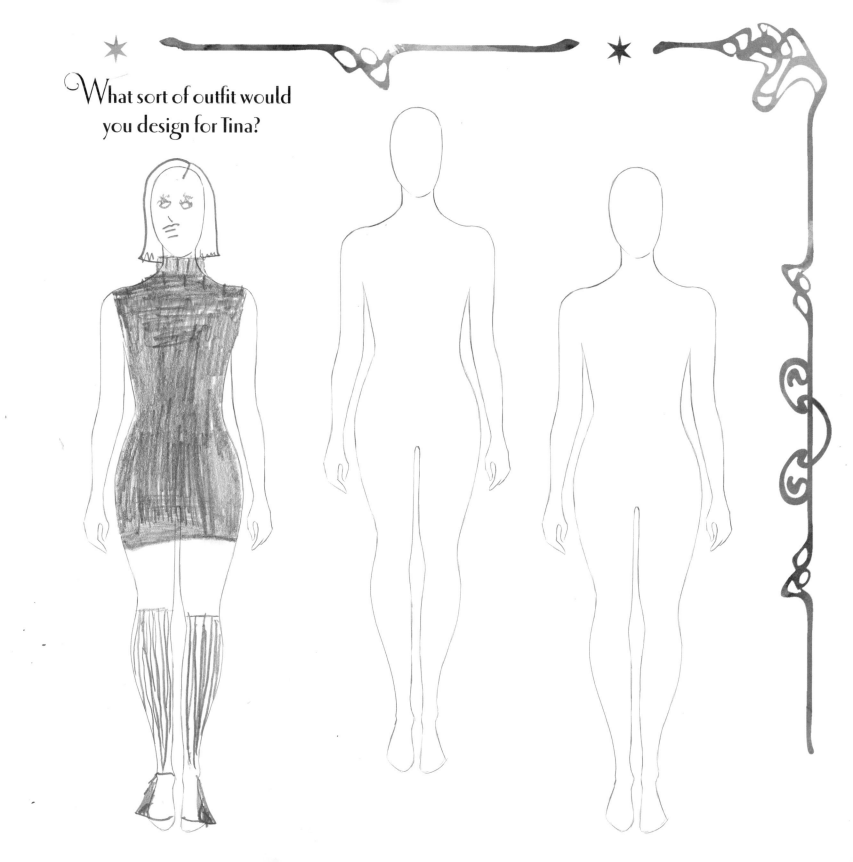

What sort of outfit would
you design for Tina?

QUEENIE GOLDSTEIN

is a glamorous and fashion-forward witch living in New York City. She and Tina are sisters.

Color and embellish Queenie's outfit.

Queenie likes to keep up with the latest trends!
What sort of stylish outfit would you design for her?

JACOB KOWALSKI

has dreams of opening his own bakery,
but first he needs to get a loan from
the bank. For his important meeting
with the bank manager, he dresses in
a three-piece suit. The suit includes a
jacket, vest, and pants.

Color and embellish Jacob's outfit.

Design what you think would make the best outfit
if you were headed to an important meeting.

Jacob wears a dark red tie with his suit.
Create and color your own patterns on the ties below.

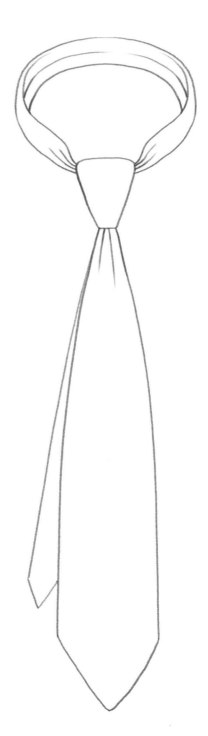

MILDRED is Jacob's fiancée. But when she finds out Jacob did not get the bank loan, she gives him back her engagement ring. Her cheery pink outfit is a sad contrast to her and Jacob's state of affairs.

Color and embellish Mildred's outfit.

Design your own
outfit for Mildred.

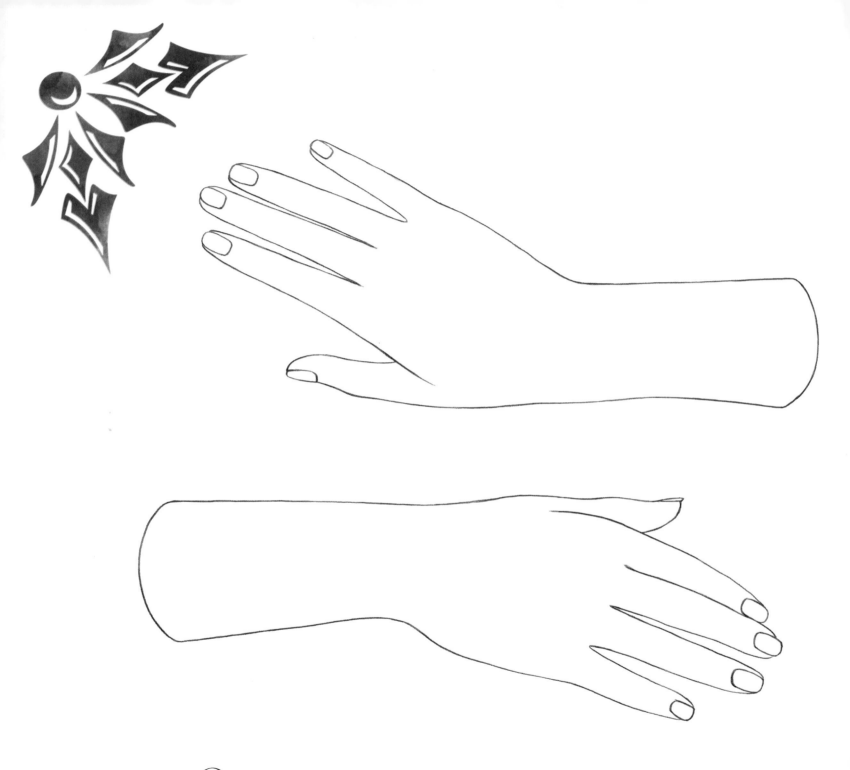

One of Newt's beasts, a Niffler, is attracted to all the shiny and sparkly rings and bracelets in jewelry store windows.

Craft your own ring and bracelet designs below. Would your jewelry attract the Niffler?

Tina and Queenie share a stylish apartment adorned with quaint decor and colorful wallpaper patterns. In their living room, Queenie keeps a dressmaker's dummy that she uses to create her own fashions using her wand.

It's your turn! Design your own fashions on
the dressmaker's dummies below.

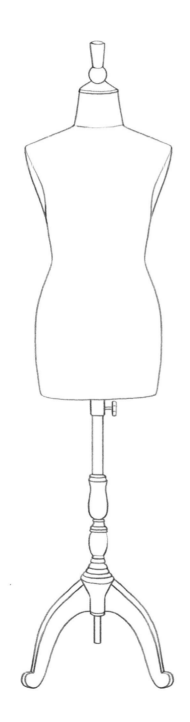
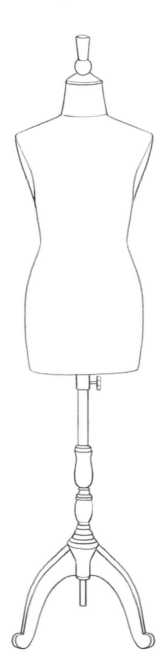
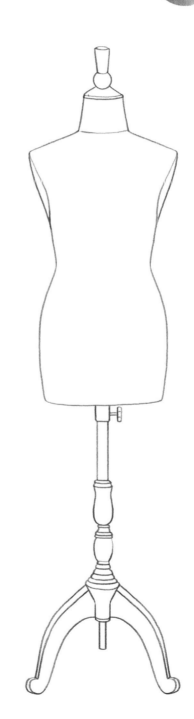

Queenie uses lots of different materials and
colorful fabrics in her dressmaking.

Design your own patterns on the swatches below.

Witches have magical products that they use to help
make everyday life easier—and more beautiful.

Design and color your own bottles and jars below.

Create a soft daytime look on Queenie by drawing light makeup below.

Create a dynamic nighttime look on Queenie by drawing dark makeup above.

Design your own winter fashions on the models below.

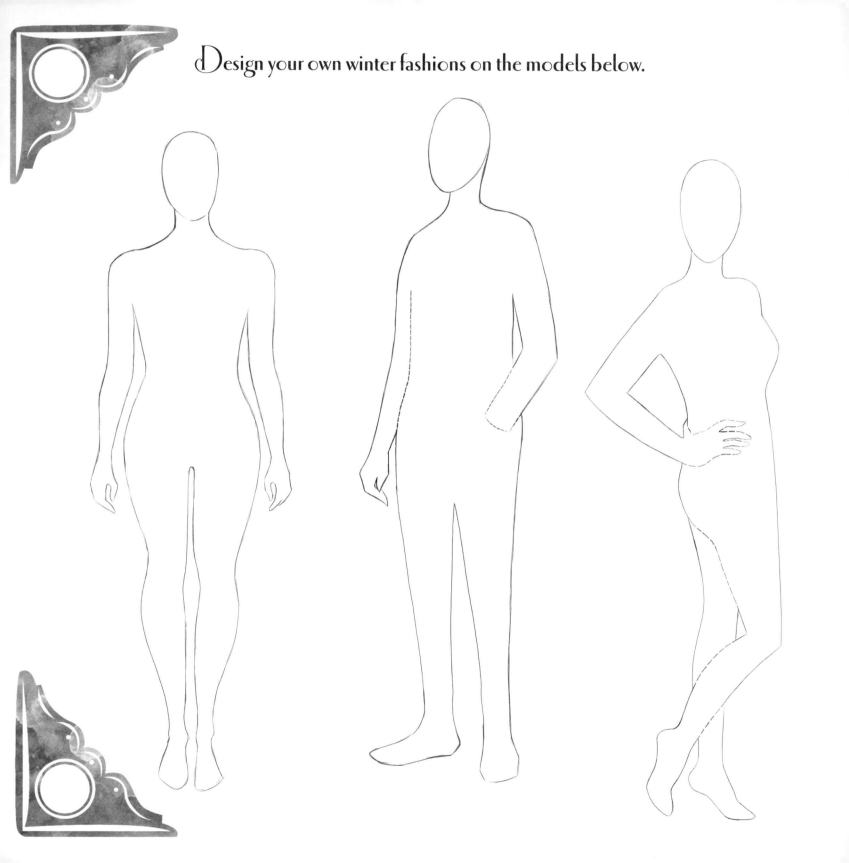

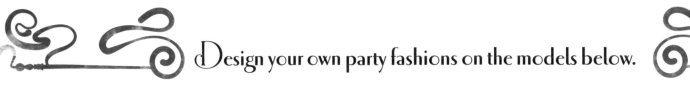Design your own party fashions on the models below.

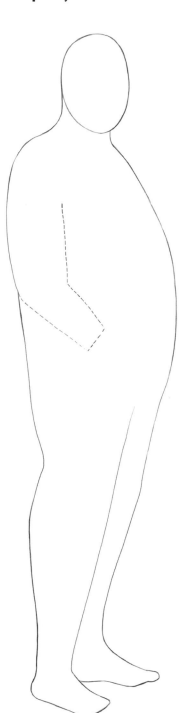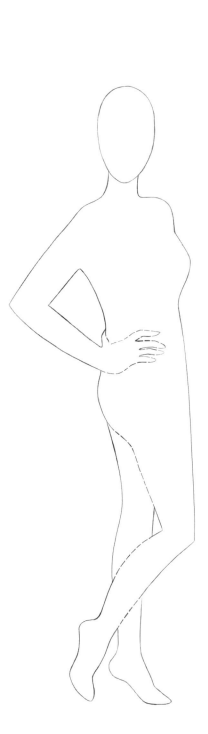

Color and embellish these women's
shoe styles from the 1920s.

Queenie's short curls are
high style for the time period.
Create and color your own hairstyle below.

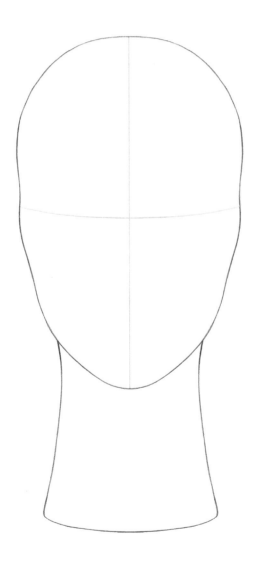

TINA makes Newt and Jacob stay at her apartment so they don't get into any more trouble on the streets of New York. That night, she wears light blue pajamas with a floral pattern to bed.

Color and embellish Tina's pajamas.

Design your own pajamas for Tina.

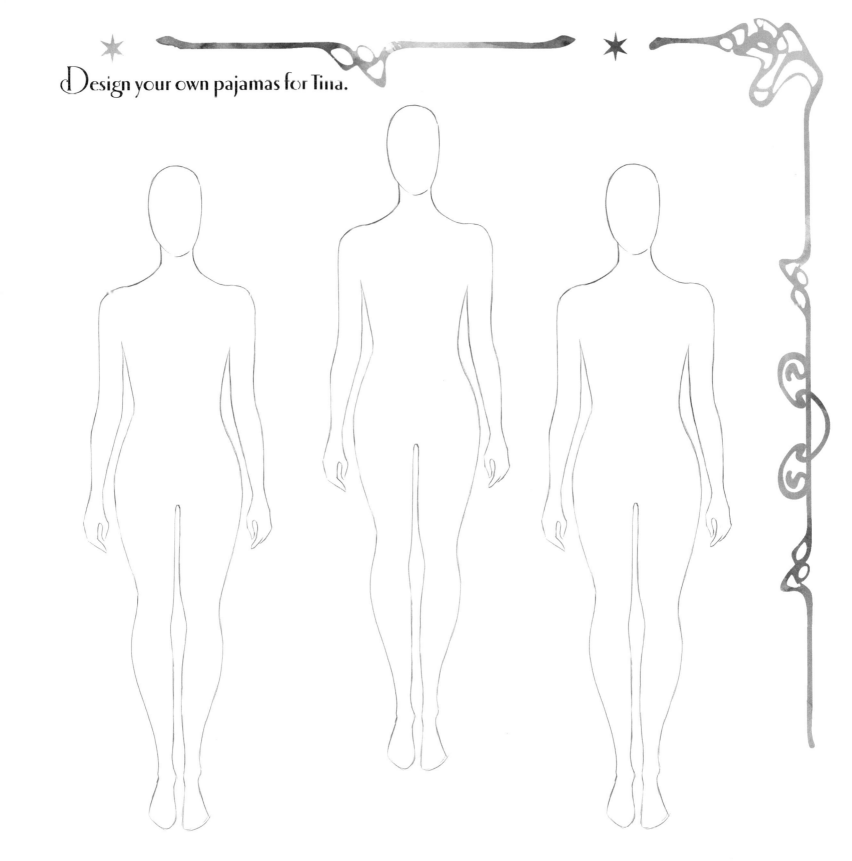

QUEENIE even looks fashionable at bedtime! She sleeps in a pink nightgown with white lace trim. A silky pink robe finishes off her look.

Color and embellish Queenie's pajamas.

Design your own
pajamas for Queenie.

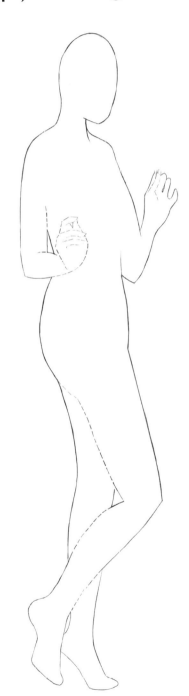

Design your own chic city fashions on the models below.

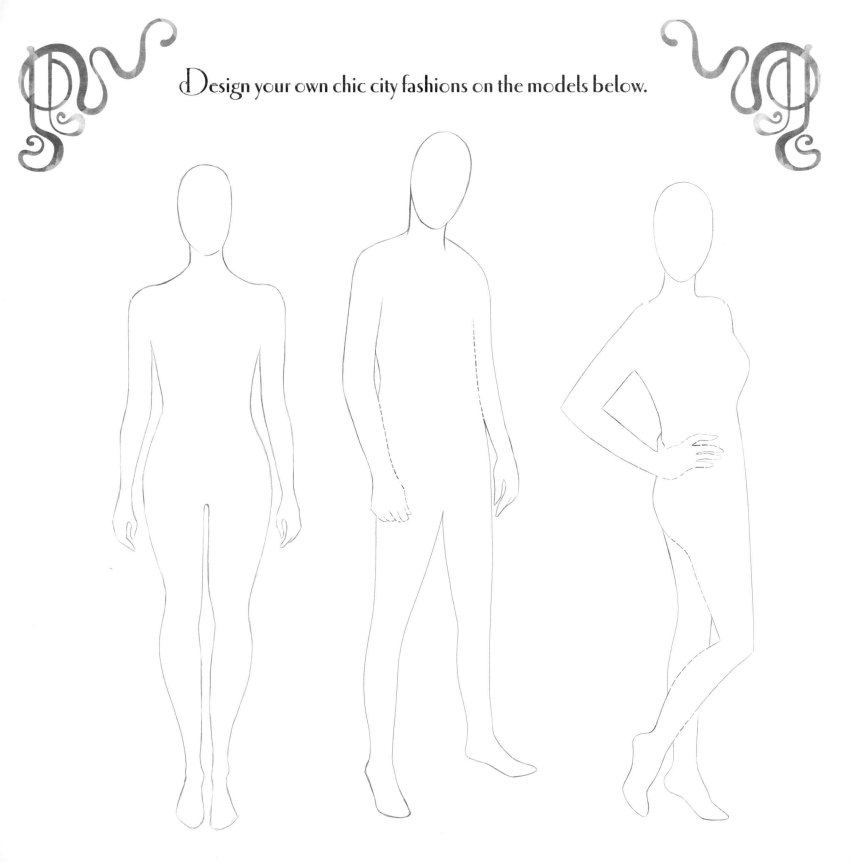

Design your own summer fashions on the models below.

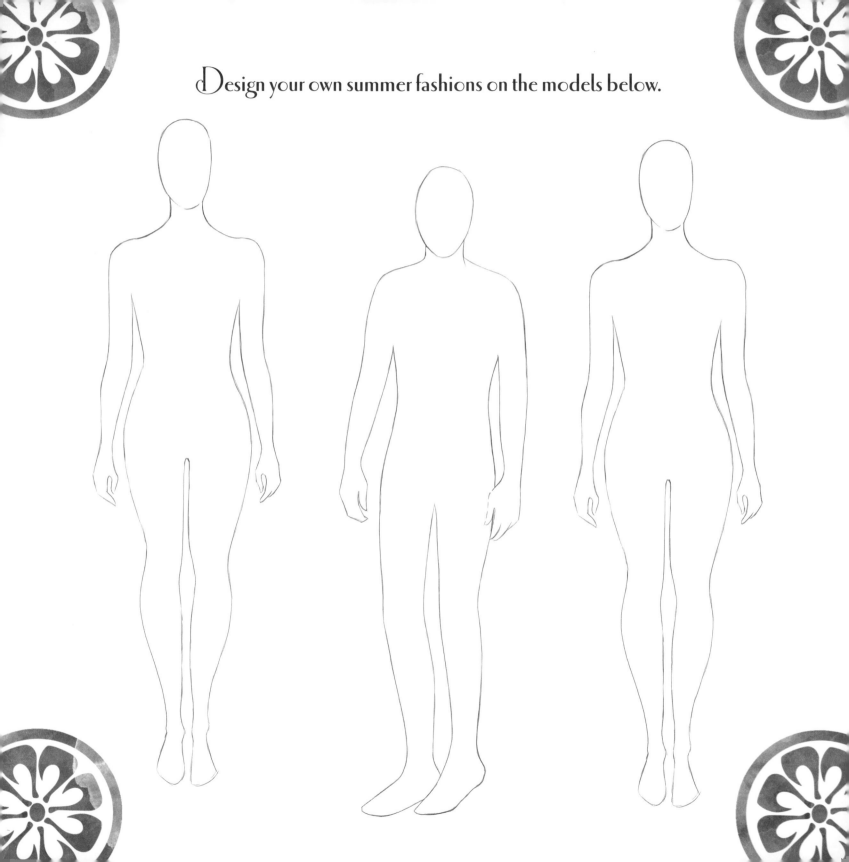

SERAPHINA PICQUERY

is the President of MACUSA. When an assembly
is in session, she wears a sleek black robe and a
matching golden headpiece.

Color and embellish Seraphina's outfit.

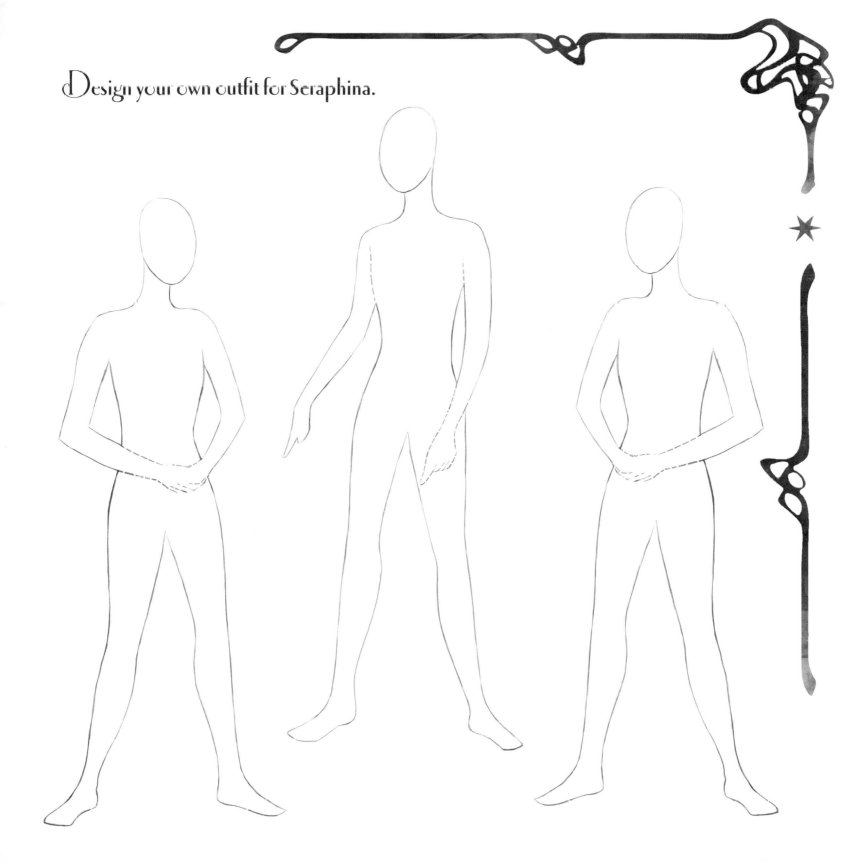

Design your own outfit for Seraphina.

Finger waves were a very popular
hairstyle for women in the 1920s.
Create and color your own hairstyles below.

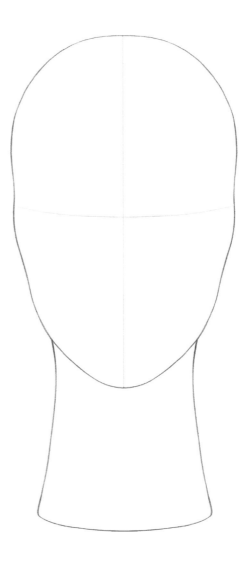

PERCIVAL GRAVES

is Director of Magical Security at MACUSA. He always dresses to impress, and his commanding black clothing matches his authoritative presence.

Color and embellish Graves's suit.

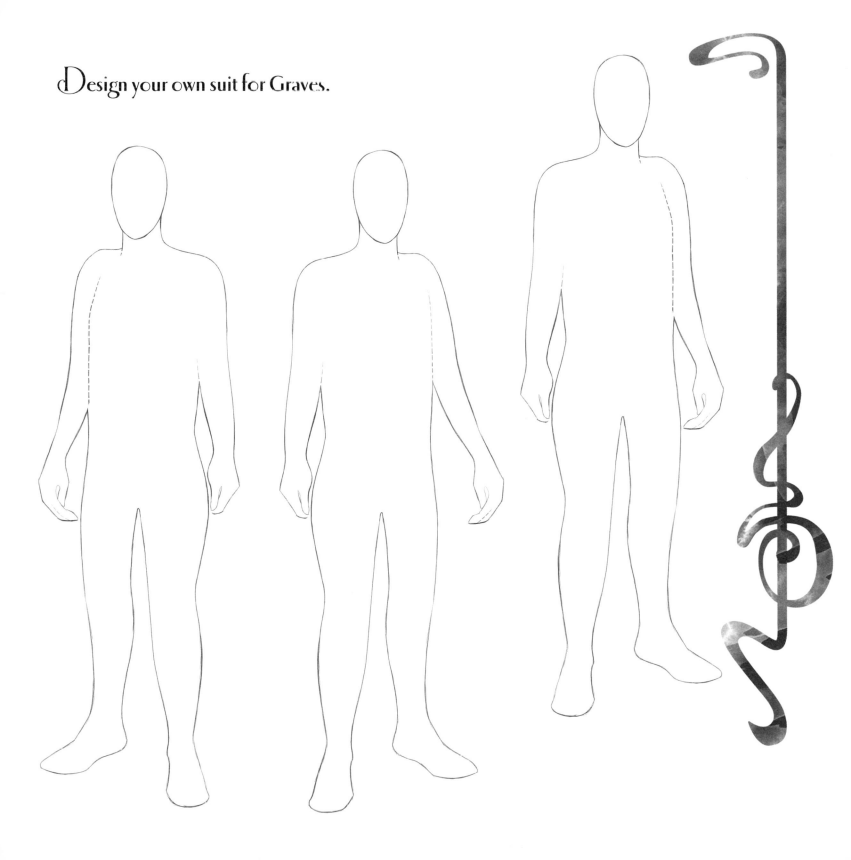

Design your own suit for Graves.

Design and color your own patterns on the vests below.

MARY LOU is the leader of
the New Salem Philanthropic Society.
She hates witchcraft, and her stern
philosophies match her dark clothing
and severe appearance.

Color and embellish Mary Lou's outfit.

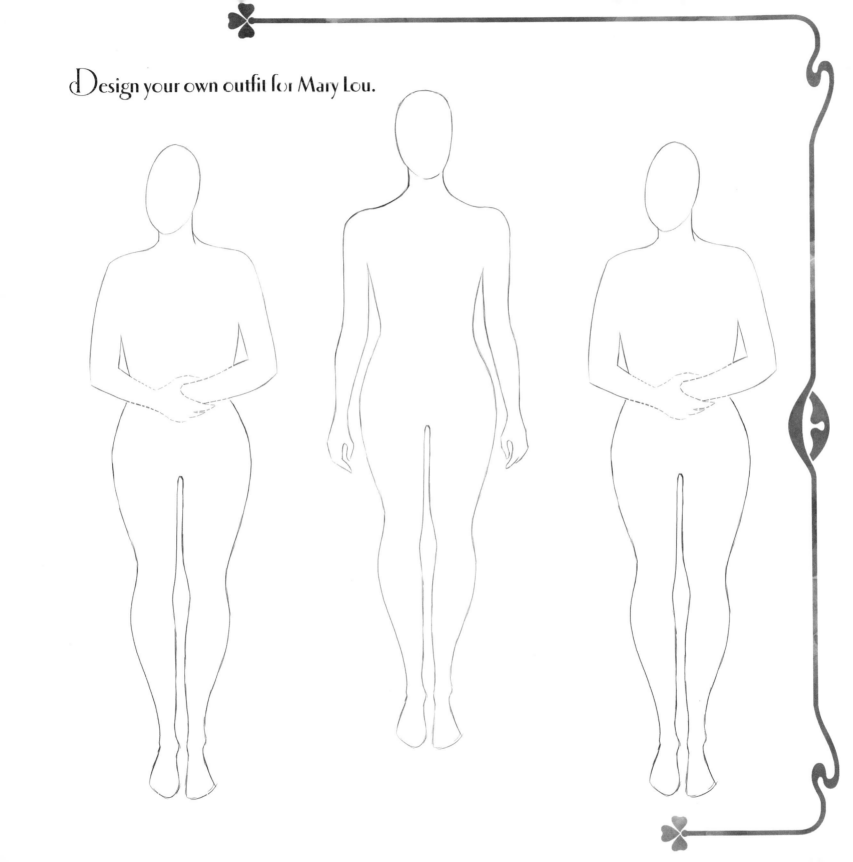

Design your own outfit for Mary Lou.

CREDENCE, Mary Lou's adopted son, wears dark, simple clothing that befits his role as a member of the New Salem Philanthropic Society.

Color and embellish Credence's suit.

Design your own suit for Credence.

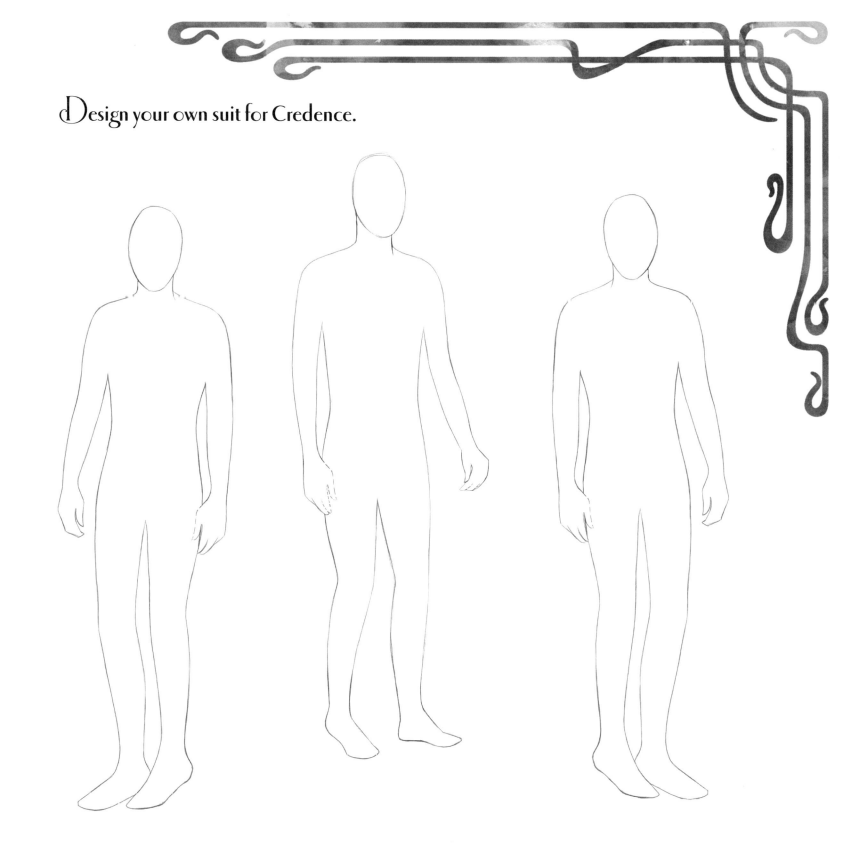

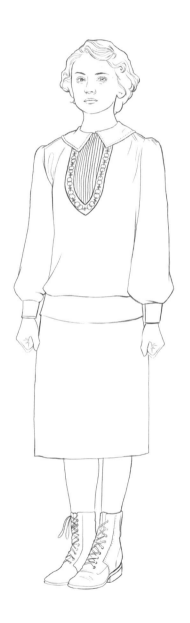

CHASTITY also participates in her adopted mother's society and wears basic, unadorned clothing, like her older brother, Credence.

Color and embellish Chastity's dress.

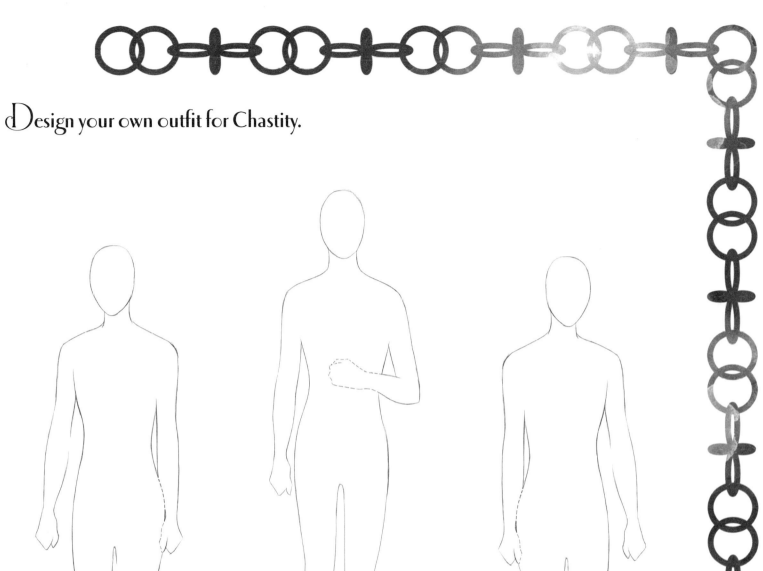

Design your own outfit for Chastity.

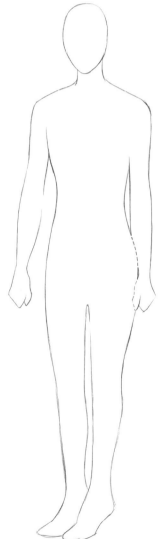

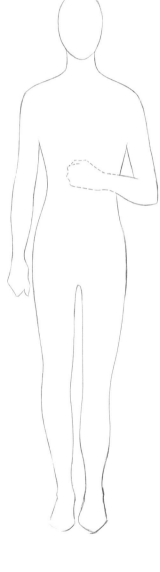

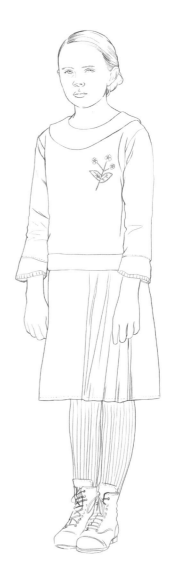

MODESTY, the youngest adopted daughter of Mary Lou, wears drab gray clothing. The only embellishment on her garment is a cluster of embroidered flowers, which are hardly cheery.

Color and embellish Modesty's outfit.

Design your own outfit for Modesty.

Color and embellish these men's hat styles from the 1920s.

Draw your own hats below.

Henry Shaw Jr.

is a politician running for reelection to the United States Senate. He makes sure his clothing is always starched and pressed to give him a polished public appearance.

Color and embellish Henry Jr.'s outfit.

Design your own outfit for Henry Jr.

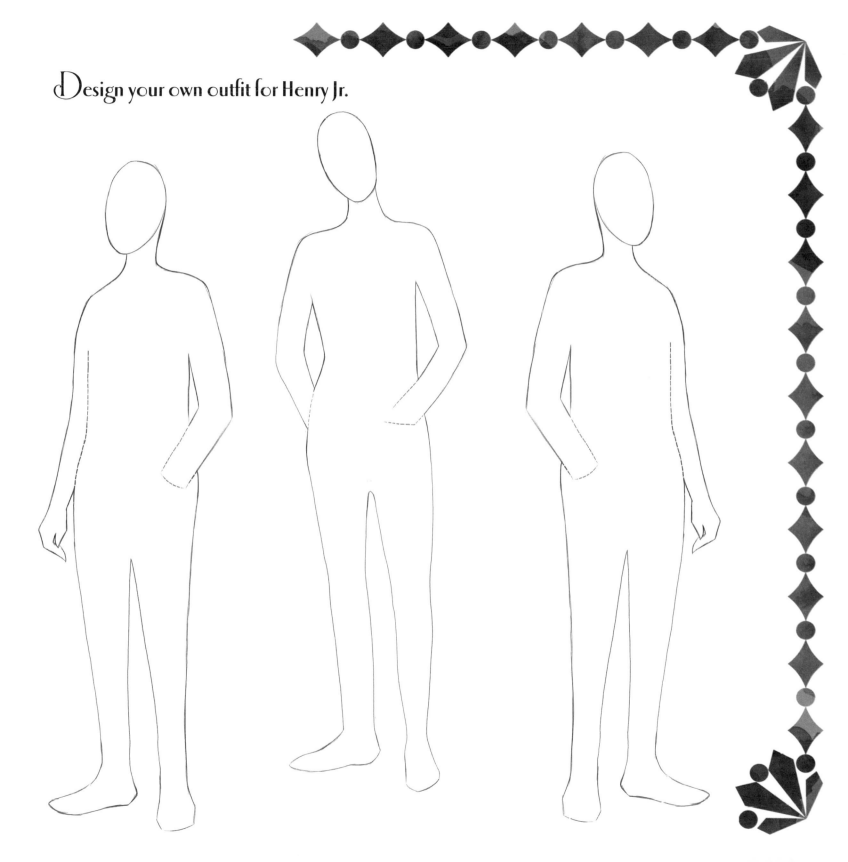

Color and embellish these men's shoe styles from the 1920s.

LANGDON SHAW is

a member of the prominent Shaw family, but his influence does not extend beyond the family name. He doesn't wear the same refined clothing of his brother and father, instead favoring more simple suits.

Color and embellish Langdon's outfit.

Design your own outfit for Langdon.

QUEENIE always makes sure that her outfit is perfectly accessorized. When it's cold outside, she wears a pink coat with an oversized velvet collar and matching hat.

Color and embellish Queenie's outfit.

Design your own outfit for Queenie.

Color and embellish these women's
hat styles from the 1920s.

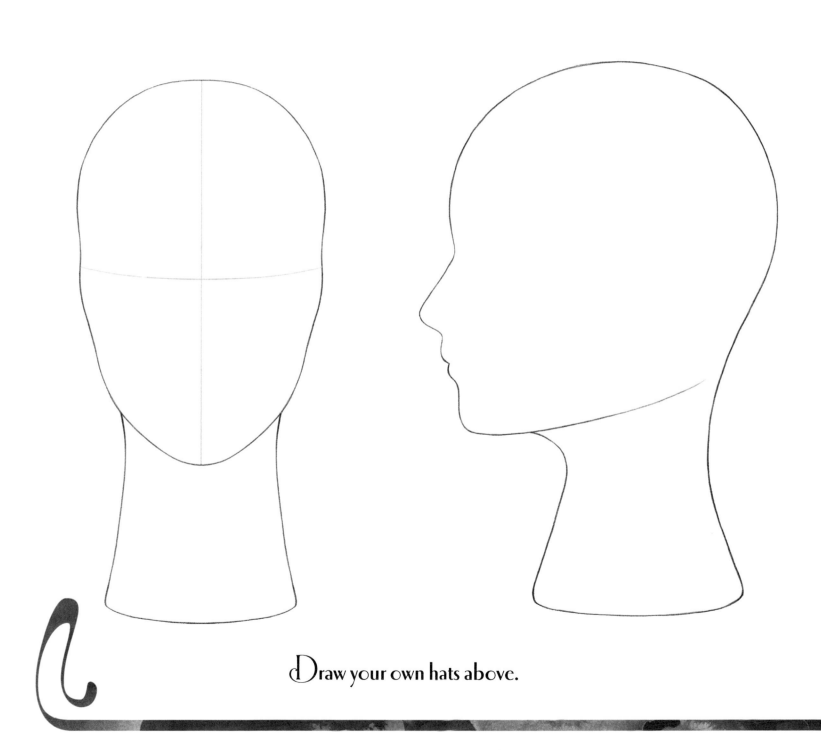

$\mathcal{D}$raw your own hats above.

Design your own fashions for a big
night out on the models below.

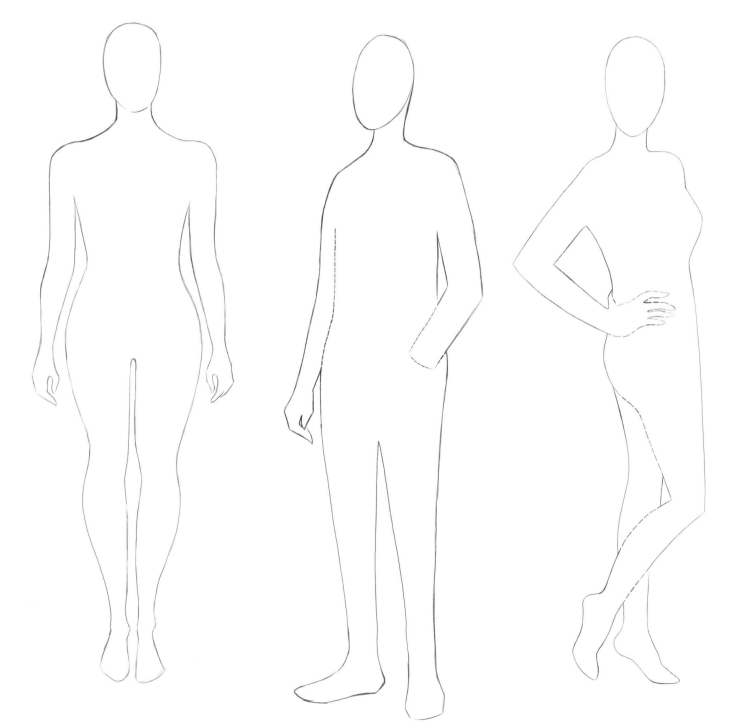

Design your own fashions for a big night
out on the models below.

During the 1920s, many women styled their hair with one curl on their face, known as a kiss curl.
Create and color your own hairstyles below.

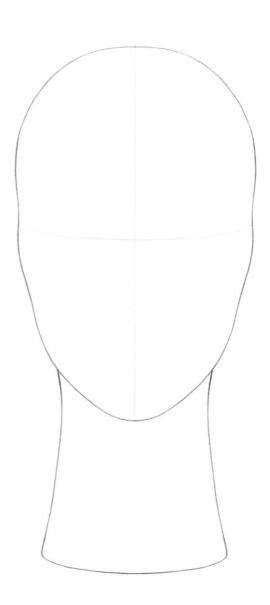

Jewelry from the 1920s often incorporated trends from the time period, such as geometric designs and patterns.

Design your own necklaces on the stands below.

Necklines during the 1920s were often very ornate, with lots of beads, sequins, and straps.

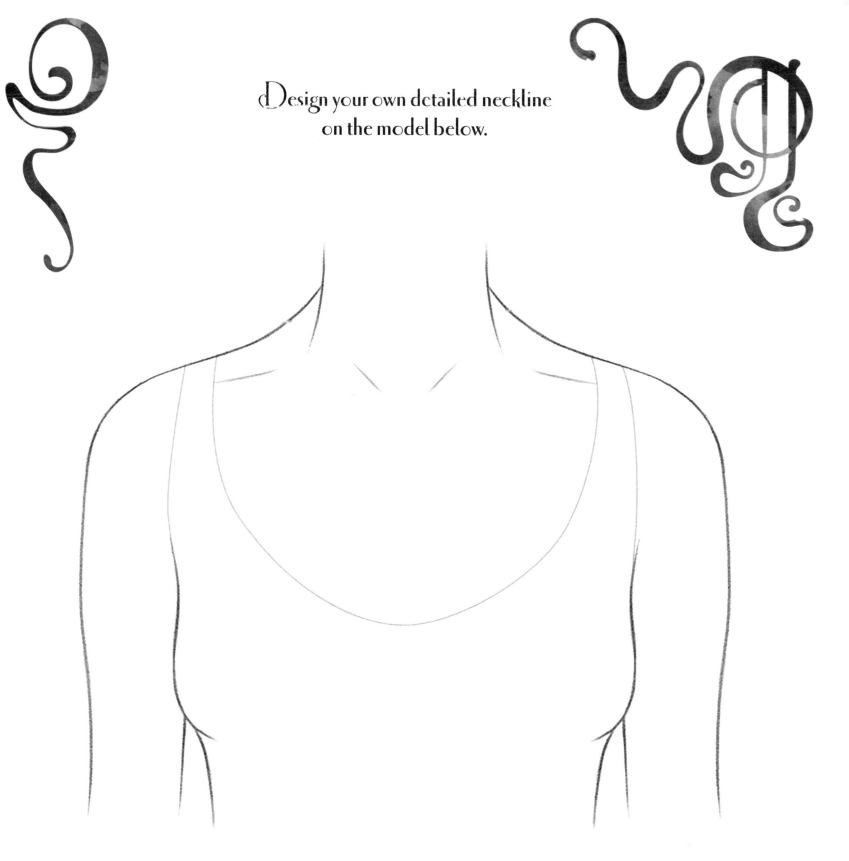

Design your own detailed neckline
on the model below.

Add hair accessories like barrettes, pins, and headbands to the styles below.

Every witch and wizard needs her or his own wand to cast magic spells.

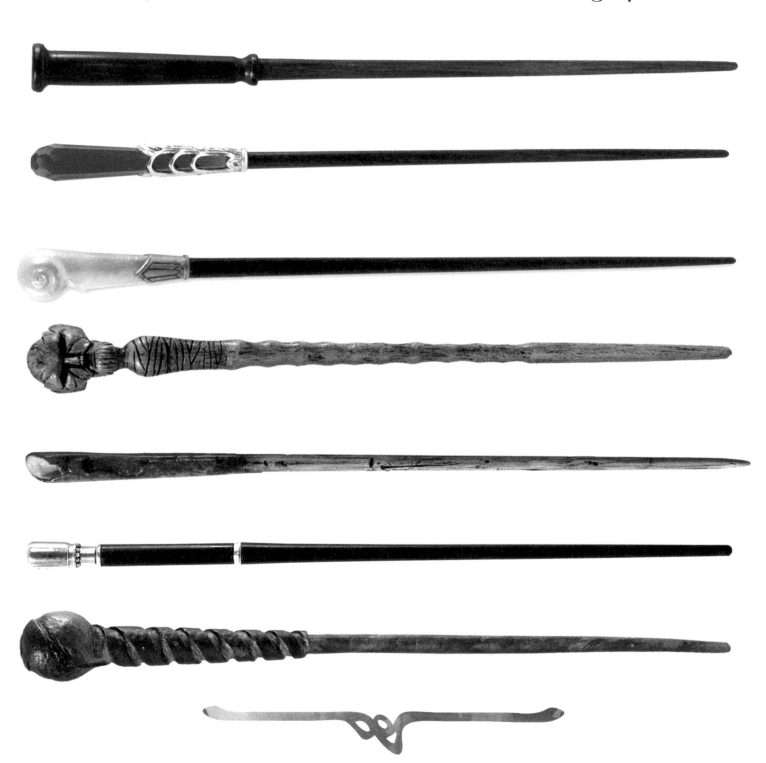

Draw your own wand below.

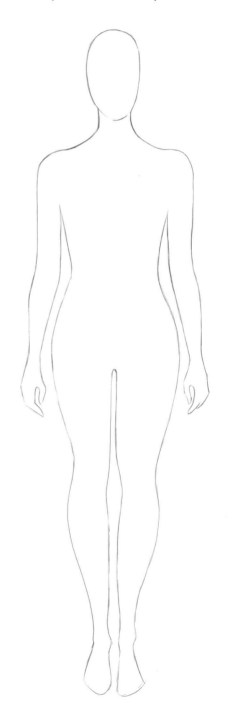

Design an outfit inspired
by the Occamy.

THE OCCAMY

is a plumed serpent with lustrous,
iridescent feathers. Its two large
wings are reminiscent of a dragon.

Design an outfit inspired
by the Billywig.

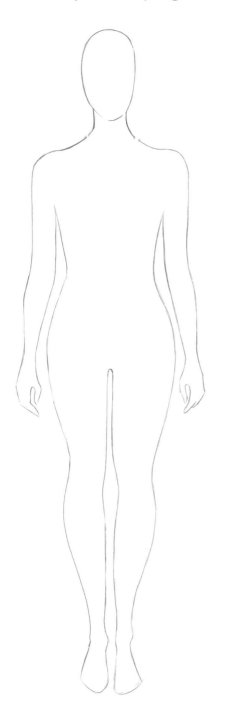

THE BILLYWIG has

a body that is a deep and brilliant

blue, the color of sapphires.

Design an outfit inspired
by the Doxy.

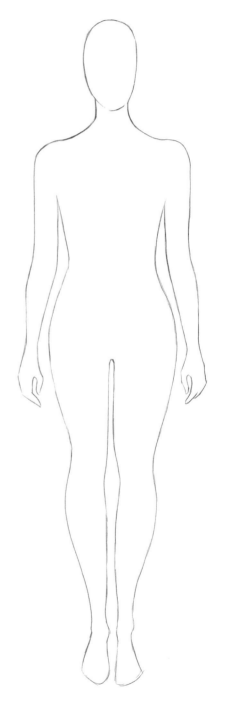

THE DOXY has bulbous
compound eyes and the scaly skin of a
lizard that changes colors to fit mood or
environment. Long, multicolored ears
fan out from its head.

Design an outfit inspired
by the Niffler.

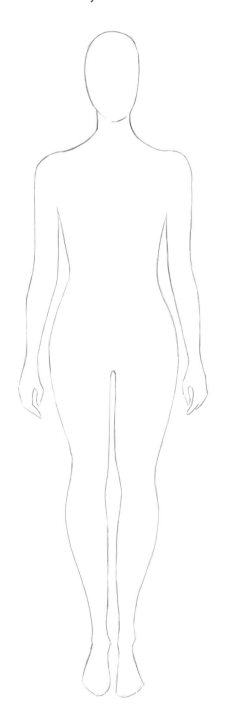

THE NIFFLER has bright,
beady eyes, dark fur, and a ducky,
flesh-colored bill like a platypus.

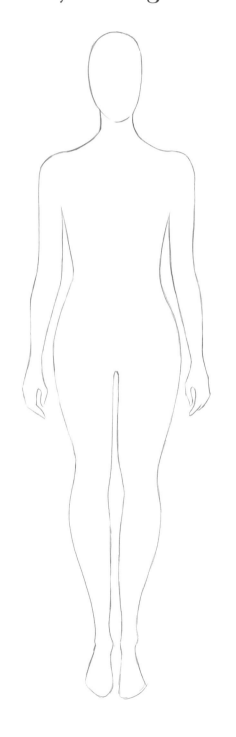

Design an outfit inspired
by the Demiguise.

THE DEMIGUISE has long
silver-white hair and doleful brown eyes,
which gives it the appearance of an old,
wise sage.

Design an outfit inspired
by the Fwooper.

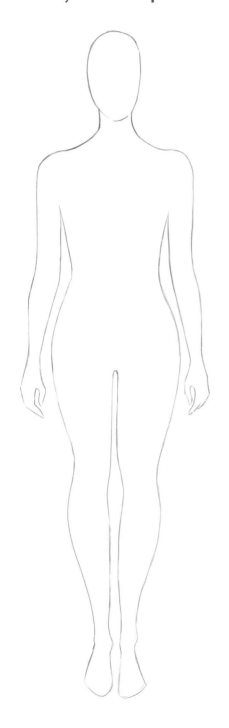

THE FWOOPER is a small

bird-like beast with delicate purple feathers

that can consume giant hunks of meat in

one bite.

THE THUNDERBIRD

THE THUNDERBIRD is an aquiline beast with six wings on its majestic body. It arranges its four sets of feathers in such a way as to present dazzling images of the sun and sky.

THE SWOOPING EVIL

THE SWOOPING EVIL has a spiked and scaly reptilian body, complete with a skull-like head and fierce fangs. Its wings possess the vibrant blue coloration of a moth or butterfly.

Design an outfit inspired
by the Thunderbird.

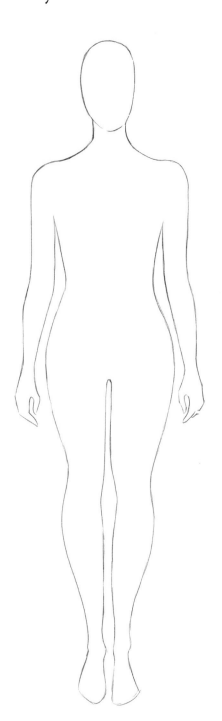

Design an outfit inspired
by the Swooping Evil.

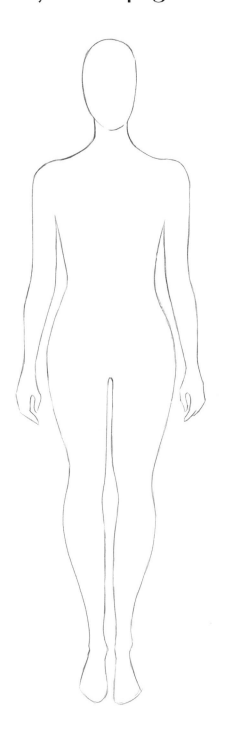